THE LIFE AND TIMES OF CHEDDI JAGAN

by

Eric L. Huntley

First Published in 1994 by Bogle-L'Ouverture Press Ltd.
P.O Box 2186.
London. W.13 9Z

ISBN 0904 521 990

Printed by The Ipswich Book Company, Suffolk

Cover design by Turu Pomel
Illustrations on pages 6, 14, 19, 21, 35, 39, 41, 68 and 86 by
Jason Brooks
Reproductions – various pages 9, 12, 24, 45, 48, 57, 63, 74

Acknowledgements

I wish to thank a number of persons who so generously gave of their time to read, comment on and encourage the progress of these pages. Professor Andrew Salkey, Dr. Frank Williams, Mrs Janet Jagan, Janice Shinebourne, Dr. Harry Goulbourne, Arif Ali of the Caribbean Times, Toks Williams, editor of the Biographical Series and in particular, a special thanks to Frank Birbalsingh who was the first to jolt the author into an awareness of the need to go back to the drawing board and to Joyce Trotman who patiently took me through the rigours of the journey.

The biographical series was first conceived by Jessica Huntley who has kept the idea alive through her continuous and painstaking support.

Lastly, without the unselfish and pioneering contribution of Cheddi and Janet and of course the people of Guyana, there would have been no story to tell.

About the Author

Eric Huntley was a founder member of the People's Progressive Party. Prior to his departure from Guyana in 1956 he was actively involved in the political destiny of that country. All the participants in the events in Guyana up to that time were known to him. He has co-authored with Eusi Kwayana, A Tribute To Paul Robeson published by the Friends of Bogle and has written two other biographies, Marcus Garvey and Two Lives - sketches of the lives of two Victorian heroines, Florence Nightingale and Mary Seacole. The author has been resident in the United Kingdom for many years and together with his wife, Jessica, has been both publisher and bookseller.

Contents

Cheddi's Birthplace

INTRODUCTION

Cheddi Jagan is one of the outstanding sons of the West Indies. The story of his life and times began in England during the 19th century, continues in India, the land of Cheddi's ancestors, and on to Guyana, the land of his birth.

One of England's best known 19th century writers, Charles Dickens, author of The Tale of Two Cities , published in 1859, described the period as, 'the best of times and the worst of times'.

Many of the inventions like gas, electricity and radio, which we take for granted today, were all developed during the latter half of the 19th century.

These inventions and other advances enabled Britain to conquer lands in Africa, Asia and the West Indies. So vast was the Empire ruled by Britain that it was said '. . the sun would never set on it'.

In India, Britain was at first able to extend its hold through two officers of the East India Company ,Robert Clive and Warren Hastings, then later by direct rule of the Colonial Office in London. During this later period, Queen Victoria assumed the title, Empress of India, together with possession of the coveted Koh-i-nor diamond of India.

The profits from this expansion overseas made many people in Britain exceedingly rich while others became poorer. Thousands were made homeless, others were forced to work long hours under terrible conditions.

Many people were hanged for minor offences, such as stealing or transported to Australia against their will.

The poor in India, like the poor in Britain, fared little better. A series of famines and plagues during the last quarter of the 19th century caused the deaths of 32 million people, more than the entire population of England at that time.

The choice for many in India was either to migrate or starve. Over two million people eventually migrated. One of the countries to which many went was British Guiana, as it was then known.

Of the two million, thousands went to East and South Africa,Fiji, Surinam and the West Indies.

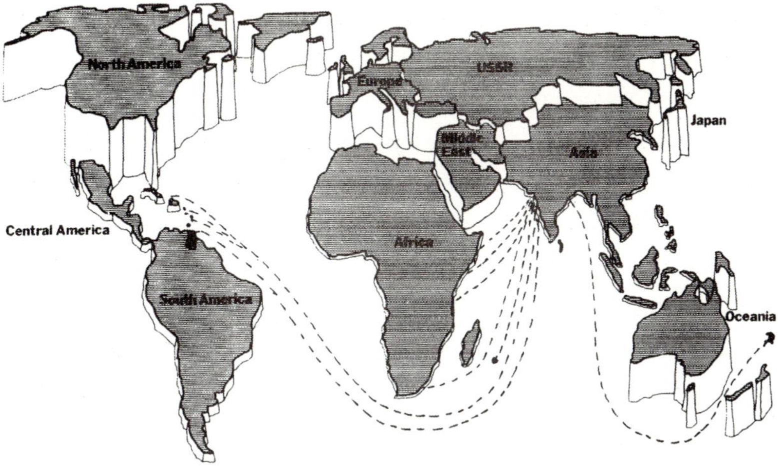

Map Showing Countries to which indentured labourers were sent

CHAPTER 1
SLAVES WIN THEIR FREEDOM

When Europeans first invaded the coast of the Guyanas, two of the main peoples they met were the Arawaks and the Wai-Wai.

The native people of Guyana resisted all attempts to enslave them. As the Europeans advanced on their territory they left the coast and went to live further away,deep into the forest regions. Europeans found it better to trade with them. With the introduction of sugar cane by Christopher Columbus to the region , the demand for labour became so great that the estate owners turned to Africa for labour to cultivate the lands. The estate owners had a great advantage in that they did not pay wages to their workers, many of whom were enslaved and taken from Africa against their will.

However, no one would work for nothing, at least not for ever. There were constant revolts by the slaves against their living and working conditions and for freedom, wages and land of their own.

Two of the most serious revolts occurred in 1763 in Berbice and in 1823 in Demerara, two counties into which Guyana was divided.

In England, many people came together and founded the Anti-Slavery Society for the abolition of the trade in slaves and the system of slavery itself.Prominent members of this Society were William Wilberforce, Thomas Clarkson and Thomas Buxton.

The campaign waged by the Society, together with the revolts of the slaves for abolition, eventually forced the British government into making the trade in slaves and slavery, illegal.

The law provided compensation to owners of estates for the loss of their labour. While the new workers were only given their freedom and nothing for the years of their enslavement.

India Rescues the Sugar Industry

After slavery was abolished, Africans left the estates and built villages of their own. Many of them chose to live as independent farmers rather than give their labour to the former slave owners.

Estate owners were therefore faced with a shortage of labour. They also had to pay wages and looked around for a cheap supply of workers.

At first, the estate owners imported workers from Hong Kong, and Madeira. Both attempts failed to satisfy the demands of the industry for labour. The reasons for this were due to the nature of the work as well as the climate. In addition, the demand for labour was too great for Hong Kong and Madeira to supply. It was left to India to come to the rescue of the sugar industry.

Planters on the island of Mauritius in the Indian Ocean, facing a shortage of labour had solved the problem by importing labour on contract from India. The success of

William Wilberforce Addressing An Anti-Slavery Meeting

this experiment encouraged sugar planters in Guyana to do likewise. The first shipment of indentured labour from India arrived in Guyana on May 5, 1838 on board two ships, the Whitby and the Hesperus with a cargo of 396 women, men and children.

Many East Indians, as they were known in Guyana were contracted to work on the estates owned by John Gladstone, father of William Gladstone, later to become Prime Minister of Britain.

Eighty years later, that token work force of 396 people had become a quarter of a million, as more and more people were transported from India across the seas to Guyana.

East Indian Migrants Arriving in Guyana

CHAPTER 2
THE STORY OF MIGRATION

People, it seems, have always migrated. At times this may have meant going to the next village or nearest city. At other times, leaving one's country and loved ones. Periods of disaster such as famine or social unrest, caused great shifts of population from one place to another and indeed, still does.

Sometimes the reason could be very personal. A quarrel with Baba (Father) and the decision to leave is made in a fit of temper. In India, many people left their homes after being enticed to do so by agents employed by estate owners. Some were even kidnapped like many Africans during the time when there was a trade in slaves.

One of the most well-known stories is that of a Mawari mother and daughter .Both were kidnapped and found themselves at a depot in Calcutta, awaiting shipment overseas. What saved them was that they were from a very wealthy family. When news of their kidnap became known, family and friends came to their rescue and freed them.

Agents of the estate owners would visit places of pilgrimage, like the holy city of Benares, on the banks of the Ganges and seek out the lonely and dejected. People sleeping rough in the city would be ready targets.

A well-rehearsed story, promising regular work, free medical care and a house was likely to entice even the most doubtful. Later, the recruiting of agents for the estate owners became better organised. People with farming experience, many of whom were in debt to their landlords, became the most likely targets.

Whatever the reasons for leaving their own home, it never entered their minds that such a journey would take them outside their country and worse still, across the black water - or Kala Pani.

Preparing For The Crossing

Saying farewell to those we love is never pleasant; for it means leaving the family which has always been there in bad times and good times. In India, it included one's maternal grandmother, Nani, grandfather, Nana, uncles and aunties, Chacha, Kaka or Chachi, Kaki or Mause and Mausa and of course, brothers, Bahiyya and sisters, Bahini, mothers, Amman, fathers, Bapa or Dado. For many, this bond of kinship and fellowship would be cut forever.

For others, new bonds -Tehari - of friendship came to be formed on board the ship during the journey which took three to four months.

Before leaving India migrants would be given a medical check-up, food and new clothes. Each migrant was issued with a name tag to put around their neck .

It is true that the migrants, many of whom could neither read nor write, were expected to sign a contract agreeing to be indentured for five to seven years. However, no contract could ever prepare them enough for the conditions they were about to meet.

The new workers were housed in the same hovels formerly lived in by those enslaved. The hours of work were long , food was poor and the general living conditions were very bad. Indeed the estate owners and overseers with whips in hand were still in charge and treated them no different to the way slaves were treated.

The Trade In India Comes To An End

In India, when news of the terrible conditions under which workers were forced to work and live became known, the National Congress Party and its leader, Mahatma Gandhi, took up the cause and campaigned for contract labour to end.

In England, the Anti-Slavery Society and the Abolitionist Movement also took up the issue. Many people saw indentureship as a new kind of slavery. In Guyana opposition to the system was also being voiced.

Many people were of the opinion that the estate owners were using contract labour to keep wages down, while at the same time expecting the general tax- payer to foot the bill.

This general concern of many people in Guyana was helped by the support of magistrate, Sir William de Voeux and James Crosby, Immigration Agent-General, both employed by the government and who, from time to time spoke out against the injustices.

Indian indentured workers also took every opportunity to protest against the harsh conditions. They went on strike, pretended to be ill and worked slowly even though in doing so, they risked imprisonment.

Despite these concerns, the system of indentureship was to continue for eighty years. During that time the trade was suspended for a number of years while minor changes were made to the system. The trade was finally brought to an end by an Act of Parliament in 1917.

The Boston Tea Party, 1773

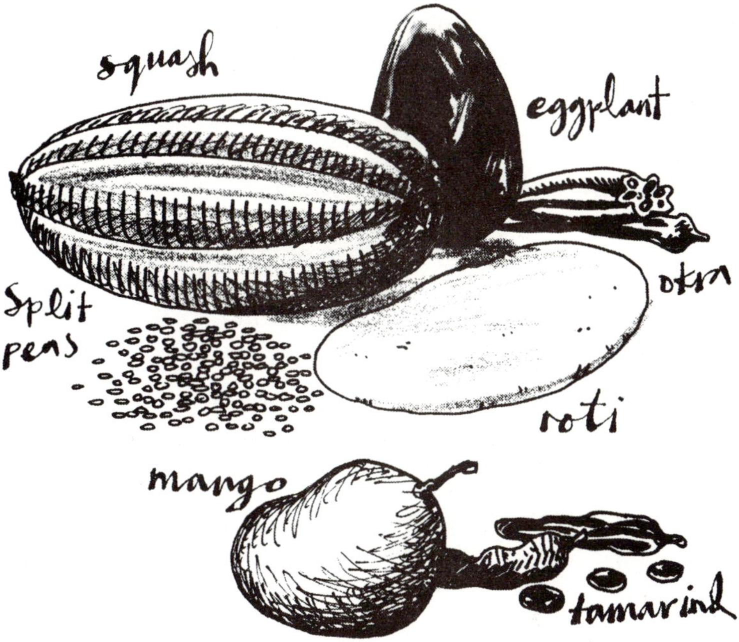

Fruits and Vegtables That Came From India

CHAPTER 3
NEW PEOPLE, NEW CULTURE

With new people a new culture came to Guyana. People express their culture in their dress, their religious practices, in the language they speak, the food they eat, their festivals and music.

Dress is perhaps what we notice first. The sari, worn by the women, the khorta, in place of the shirt and the dhoti instead of the trousers for men.

Not all the festivals from India have been kept up, and many have changed from their original form. The main festivals are Ramilila which celebrates Prince Rama ridding the world of the demon, Kaliman.

Diwali, sometimes called the festival of lights, which celebrates the goddess of wealth and good luck.

Holi or Pagwah is perhaps the most well-known festival in Guyana and is held to celebrate the spring and harvest festival.

The majority of East Indians in Guyana came from North and North-East India, in the province of Uttar Pradesh.

Many are Muslims for whom the Hosay festival is certainly the most popular.

Without music, song and dance, festivals would be dull affairs.

The tabla, sitar, tong, dentels and harmonium have all made the journey across the waters.

Plants, fruits and vegetables have also made the jour-

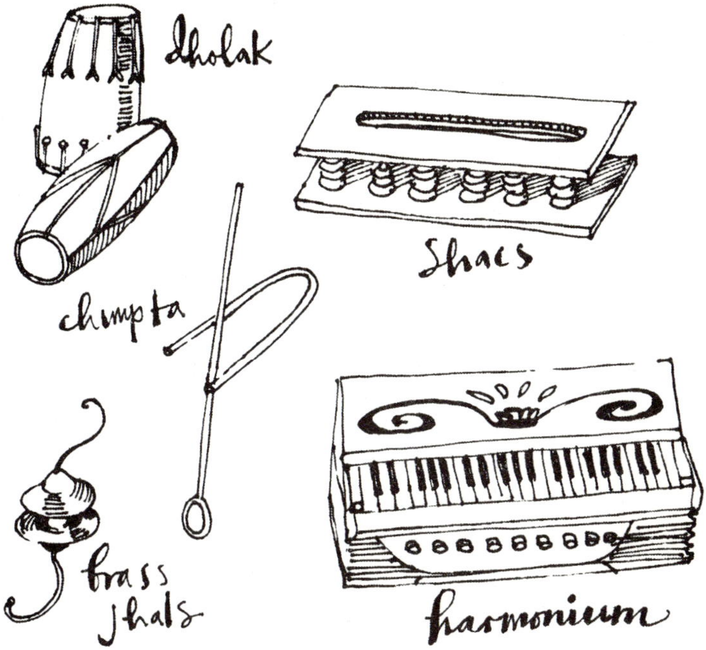

Indian Musical Instruments

ney across the waters. Some of the most well known vegetables are aam or mango, bigan or egg plant, lanki or squash, bhindi or okra.

Among those making the journey were religious leaders from India. Soon the landscape in the countryside became dotted with places of worship, temples and mosques alongside Christian churches; while Hindi words have found their way into the everyday speech of all Guyanese.

Negative Words and Images

One of the new words to have crossed the Kala Pani was Coolie. The word was used by Europeans to identify a particular tribe in India, the Kali, many of whom did manual work. In time the word came to be used as a put-down or insult to describe all East Indians.

Africans and Indians playfully call each other 'coolie' and 'black man' without the slightest feeling of bad mind or ill-feeling; however, there are times when feelings have boiled-over into violence and ill-will.

One of the main areas of conflict between the Africans and East Indians in Guyana occurred during indentureship. When Africans learnt that Indians were working for less wages than they were, they could not understand why someone would travel all the way across the Atlantic Ocean to work for so little. Africans, of course did not realise that the contracts which Indian workers had signed bound them to those conditions and set wages. What mattered to the Africans was that the Indian workers were in a position to keep wages down.

One other myth also took root during this time. Estate owners knew that the contract was for a certain number of years, they therefore worked them mercilessly. These conditions, together with a poor diet and bad sanitary conditions led to the Indians becoming ill more often than the Africans. This in turn gave rise to the myth that Indians were not as strong as Africans.

The written word has also had an adverse effect on the Indian migrants.This can be traced to English writers like Anthony Trollope and Rudyard Kipling who had come into contact with Indian society. For both writers, to be civilised one had to be a European, wear a suit and speak Standard English. Their views on Africans were of course no different. Yet many Africans in Guyana came to accept such views and also looked- down on East Indians.

On the other hand, Indians could not understand how it was that Africans had come to lose their religion, dress and language and to adopt those of Europeans. So another myth took root in the minds of the Indians: that Africans had no culture of their own. However, by working and living side by side the two communities were able to share, respect and enjoy each other's traditions, though with occasional outbursts of prejudice.

Thatched huts built on the ground were later replaced by houses built on stilts to keep out flood waters.

The Ship *'Elbe'* Sails for Guyana

It was against this background that in 1901 Cheddi Jagan's grand- parents set sail. In doing so they joined many thousands of their countrymen and women who had made the journey.

Of course not only men and women made the journey but also children and even babies. Indeed, some were born on board the ships, others shortly after arriving in Guyana. Cheddi's father arrived at the age of two. His mother was eighteen months old.

Their correct dates and years of birth were not recorded as it was not the practice to do so at that time. The exact locations of their places of birth is not known. It is thought however, that they came from Basti in the Province of Uttar Pradesh, about sixty miles from the city of Allahabad, Jawaharlal Nehru's birthplace.

We will never know for certain what were the reasons which caused his grandparents to make the journey across the Kala Pani.

If Cheddi's grandparents had not migrated he would have been part of an extended family network, including several uncles, aunts, nieces and nephews and cousins.

Growing up in Guyana his immediate family consisted of just five persons, two grandmothers, his father, mother and an uncle on his father's side. All came as indentured immigrants in 1901.

CHAPTER 4
PORT MOURANT ESTATE

The Atlantic seashore of Berbice was parcelled into lots. Port Mourant was lot ten. To this day, many villages along the coast are known simply by their number along this coastal chain.

Early European settlers were well aware of the healthy breeze coming from the Atlantic and compared the freshness of the air with that of Barbados.

For the majority of workers the cooling effects of the Atlantic Ocean breeze hardly mattered. What moulded their lives were, the public road, the cane fields, the sugar mill, the manager and the yards where they lived.

The Atlantic Ocean might as well have been thousands of miles away. Due to the rough currents of the ocean no port was built and an outlet to the sea was provided only by canal to the Canje Creek at the backlands of the estate.

The estate comprised Port Mourant, Tain, Clifton and Jones combining cotton and sugar production during the nineteenth century. Originally bought by Stephen Mourant in 1820, it changed ownership several times, finally becoming part of the Booker and McConnell group of companies during the 1950s.

The estate was described by Cheddi in his book, The West On Trial as the 'hub of life'. Everything revolved around the production of sugar. Some villages, towns and even cities are like that even today. Bauxite mining districts like McKenzie and Kwakwani in Guyana, naval and army dockyards at Dover and university towns like Cambridge are sometimes so organised that most aspects of people's lives revolve around that one activity.

The Estate Manager

The manager of the estate, J.C. Gibson, was very powerful and his word was law not only on matters to do with the estate but also the surrounding villages.

His word influenced the decisions of the courts, the doctor, the water supply, education and of course, who was to be hired or fired. Workers were expected to take their hats off as a sign of respect when Mr. Gibson passed-by.Needless to say when he was seen coming the workers simply vanished rather than bow to him.

Despite the poor working and living conditions the estate did not seem to be affected by major labour disputes. The social pyramid placed the manager at the pinnacle. He lived in a mansion or manor house. Next were the overseers. They lived in smaller mansions, all painted lily-white, fenced off from each other with spacious grounds and well-kept lawns. Other monthly-paid staff such as office workers lived in a settlement apart.

At the bottom of the ladder were the Indian and African workers who lived in hovels in yards known as the 'free yard', 'nigger yard' and 'bound yard'.

Living conditions in these yards were worse than those of any worker in free villages or in towns, worse than

Albouystown, one of the poorest wards in the city of Georgetown. Housing was mainly hovels, built using local materials, with for example, some walls made of 'wattle', roofs from 'trollie' grass and other walls plastered with a mixture of the dung of cows and earth.

There was no running water and a trench which passed between the houses , served as the water supply for all purposes. Foreign visitors to the estate very often mistook the hovels in which the workers lived for the stables in which the horses were kept.

The stables for both mules and horses were lighted by electricity while the homes of the workers were lit by kerosene lamps. It was generally felt that more care was taken of mules and horses than of the workers.

CHAPTER 5
FAMILY LIFE

Cheddi's Mother

Writing of his mother Cheddi had this to say, 'she tackled the more routine and difficult task of balancing the family's budget. . .'

His mother as seen by an outsider, Martin Carter, the poet, who met her during the fifties, recalled ' a gentle, almost wraith-like [woman], who spent her life keeping her children alive . . . literally alive'.

A mainly vegetarian diet of dhal made from lentils, bhaji or spinach, and rice was hardly enough nourishment to sustain a healthy body which bore eleven children.

Mother Jagan was a devout Hindu and her religious beliefs were a great source of strength and support. Her belief in re-incarnation made her feel that all the suffering had not been in vain.

The Black Dot

As a child, Bachoni (Cheddi's mother's first name) started work in the Creole gang. This was a team of African and Indian women and children workers. She, like others would be employed fetching earth, ashes, manure and taking care of young canes. Sometimes she was required to work at nights. A twelve-hour day was not unusual for a wage of sixty cents per week.

Few people saw anything wrong in children working. Children also worked in the textile mills and coal mines of Europe. Indeed one official in Guyana wrote that the children enjoyed working.

Child labour was also permitted because it was not compulsory to send children to school and of course education was not as yet free. Female children of East Indian parents were not expected to attend school.

Bachoni was married at the tender age of eight and a Black Dot placed on her forehead. It is doubtful if her parents could have afforded a golden toe-ring (Amant) as was the custom. When she was aged fourteen, she moved into the home of her in-laws and she and Cheddi's father lived there as man and wife.

Her first-born child, a boy, died aged eight months. This was a terrible shock for her and the family. Scores of people died during this time, due to a world-wide 'flu epidemic.

When Cheddi was born later on ,their faith and hope were renewed. A flag was raised for him and a special Puja for good luck.

By the time Cheddi was nine years old four siblings had been born and it was time for his mother to stop working on the estate.

Her Dechima Pisa Came In Handy

There was much to be done at home. Like many mothers, her work was never finished. The floors and walls of the house had to be daubed regularly and re-plastered, she had to take the clothes and gnat or scrubbing-board down to the canal to wash. Food had to be cooked and she still had to help out during the planting and reaping of the rice crop .

Since her husband worked from sun-rise to sun-setand sometimes on Saturday mornings, he was seldom at home.This placed a heavy burden on her. She not only had to tend to the children's every need, but also had to see in what way she could contribute to the income of the family.

At the time of Cheddi's birth the First World War had just ended and the export price of sugar fell, while the price of goods in the shops rose. Many workers lost their jobs.

Cheddi's mother was a very resourceful person. The kitchen garden with its bijan, okras, peppers and shallots was tended with care and during the week and on Saturdays, the produce was sold at the market. In time a cow or two and later, a few acres of land under rice-paddy cultivation all helped to bring in a few extra pennies.

In this way, many women, though they did not go out to work and bring in a wage every week, were still able to draw on their 'dechima pisa' ,loose change put aside for a rainy-day.

CHAPTER 6
CHEDDI'S FATHER

One of The Best Workers

It is four o'clock in the morning and dawn is still asleep. Mother Jagan rouses wearily as if by instinct as there is no clock in the house.

The lamp is lit and she approaches the make-shift shrine in the corner of the room, incants a silent mantra (prayer) and moves towards the low-mouth to put on a saucepan of water to make coffee or bush tea.

She allows her husband to sleep, knowing too well that he would need every ounce of his strength for the day ahead. The fire is slow to ignite, the wood is damp and smoke blows back into her face, causing her eyes to burn.

With a deftness of her fingers that only years of practice have made possible, the dough for making roti is ready and the tawa used to cook the roti on, is on the fire.

For her husband, today there will be only roti. Hopefully, the evening meal will be a bit better, some aaloo (potato) or bhoonjal curry and rice.

Before leaving, Mr. Jagan calls out to his neighbour and joins the scores of barefooted men and women trudging their way along the dam, cutlass, saucepan and kata in hand, on their way to receive their working orders for the day.

It is several miles, to the work point. By the time he

gets there he is already hungry enough to eat his breakfast but knows full well that he dares not and disciplines himself to wait until nine o'clock when it would be time to stop for a short break.

Father Jagan Earns His First Spurs

At fourteen, this tall strapping figure of a young man has earned his spurs. His first four years had proven his ability to work to instruction, fetching grass and manure to nourish the young canes and clearing the young stalks of weed, to help them on their way to healthy growth.

It was his skill as a cane-cutter which confirmed his standing in the eyes of fellow workers and overseers that here was a young man who could hold his own among the best on the estate.

As a cane-cutter the work was harder, but he also earned more money which he was able to spend on his growing family.

Even though he had spent only a mere three years in school, those lessons - the daily recitation of tables, and the alphabet, learning how to add and subtract - were to be a great help.

A staunch Hindu, he wore a churki and took part in the major religious festivals. It was however at the annual cricket matches and horse race meetings that his presence was most familiar.

Here was a young man , ambitious, hardworking and full of energy but who could only be promoted to the position of driver or a headman. A driver received orders from the overseer and passed them on to others. A driver was expected to know all the tasks workers were engaged on in the field.

There were no African or East Indian overseers. Such jobs were reserved for Europeans. The overseers were also 'bound' to work for three years and had to be taught the skills required to produce a healthy crop of sugar cane and rum by workers like Mr. Jagan.

As a driver he was placed in a very difficult position. The job opened up opportunities which were not available to the other workers. At a social level he became a more acceptable partner with the white overseers at card games. He may have suffered a loss of earnings but did not have to endure the hard work of cutting cane. The loss of earnings was made up for by his wife's good house-keeping and the income from her garden and the milk she sold .

Mr. Jagan never forgot the manual workers in the field and although he could not openly advise them on what course of action to take in the event of a dispute, he did so privately whenever this was possible.

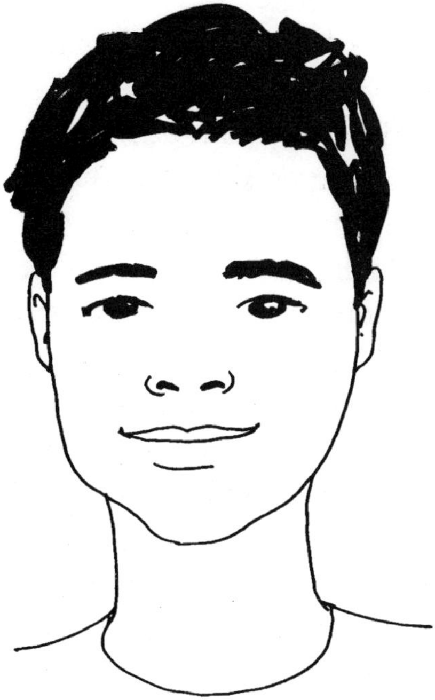

Cheddi At Age Twelve

CHAPTER 7
GROWING-UP YEARS

Education - The Key

As Cheddi grew up, the estate and its manager continued to cast their shadow over all aspects of life. However, changes were taking place. One of the major changes was in education.

Generally children in country areas were less provided for in terms of education than those in the towns. Those living on sugar estates and especially Indians were the least catered for. There were a number of reasons for this.

Estate owners were generally more concerned to have a large work-force in reserve so as to keep wages down. It was felt that once young people were educated they would leave the estate and look for jobs elsewhere. Children and women were part of this reserve. This was because everyone's wages were so low that parents relied on the income their children received.

During harvesting of rice and sugar cane the demand for labour increased and both the estate owners and parents who planted rice relied on the entire family. If you were an older girl-child in the family, you were expected to care for your younger brothers and sisters while both parents went out to work.

The custom which regarded girls simply as marriageable material, mothers and housewives, worked to their disadvantage. Their education was seen as being mainly in the home preparing them for these roles.

Cheddi Starts School

All this changed when primary education was made both compulsory and free.The Primary School which was run by the Anglican Church in Port Mourant was Cheddi's first experience of formal education.

It was not long before news had spread that Headmaster Ralph at Rosehall, the nearest village, was obtaining good results from his pupils. Cheddi soon enrolled at this school. He was able to mix with a wider cross-section of the community. The majority of children at Rosehall were Africans.

Headmaster Ralph not only helped to mould Cheddi in these early years but also became a friend of the family.

Rosehall, which was situated between the estates of Albion and Port Mourant, provided a welcome relief to the workers on the adjoining estate who could visit the market on Saturdays, enjoy a film at the cinema or a game of cricket during the season and generally relax and socialise.

Life skills learned early

As far as Cheddi's mother was concerned, training for life was not going to be restricted to book education, but would be combined with the values of home economics.

Cheddi was allowed a certain portion of the garden for his own use. He planted, reaped and sold the produce. Whatever pocket money he received had to be earned. On trips to market on Saturdays where his mother had a stall, he helped to give change and bartered with customers. This provided him with experience which no text book could give.

His arithmetic was learnt at the market stall with his mother, long before the Shilling Arithmetic text book was available

Saturday was always a treat. The market scene was a bustling one, of vendors selling eggs, fish, limes, oranges, bigan, tomatoes, okras, spinach, callaloo (kaale) plantains, peppers, mustard, ghingie and bhajee, among other produce. The market at Rosehall was a good meeting ground for the exchange of African foods, such as root vegetables like cassava and eddoes or lentils like black-eyed peas, which added variety to the daily diet.

Scrambling For Pennies

On Saturday nights his father would return home, bringing with him canned sardines and biscuits or bread and cheese. The family looked forward to these treats with relish for they provided an enjoyable change from the usual fare.

Less often, once a year on Christmas day, the manager's wife would stand on the balcony of her mansion and invite the children to scramble for pennies which she

The Holi

threw at them.

The manager's mansion was of course, out-of-bounds the rich man in his castle, the poor at the gate - however, an eight-year old could not help but marvel at the well-kept lawns, the lily-white painted mansion, the electric lights and wonder what else lay behind the closed doors.

Fire On The Holi

Living was hard, but pleasurable as Cheddi recalled. . . 'There were so many simple pleasures in the country-side. Looking at my own and other city children, I have always felt that they miss so much. Poverty had been intense at Port Mourant. Country life was full of rich experiences, perching on the fork of a tree at the centre of the Kharian , (threshing ground) prodding the oxen to urge them on their seemingly endless tramp-mashing (threshing) of padi; sleeping on padi haystacks under starry skies, even with clouds of mosquitoes buzzing around: watching cows grazing in the reaped padi fields, catching fish with hooks and cast-nets, thrusting one's hand into holes along the banks of empty trenches to find sometimes not fish, but non-poisonous water snakes, shooting birds with sling-shots, walking barefoot and pitching marbles in muddy puddles, burning the Holi - heap and playing "mud" and "abir " at Phagwah time and attending the August races.

The Port Mourant Horse and Mule Race was almost a national institution. Preparations were made for this as

The Pagwah

if for a great festival. New clothes were purchased, shoes bought by those who had never worn any before and white yachtings (sneakers) were bravely worn though invariably by the end of the day they were either strung around one's neck or carried home under one's arm.'

Observing Traditional And Religious Customs

Cheddi, as the eldest son of a hardworking cane-cutter was also a Hindu who had to keep certain customs.

One of these was to wear an ear-ring. Another was to have his head shaved on the thirteenth day after the death of his paternal grandmother. Keeping-up both these traditions led to his being teased by school mates.

The annual Hindu festivals of Holi, Deepavali, Kalimai Puja and Ram Leela were exciting and enjoyable, especially the Holi .

For this occasion, Cheddi and his young friends would spend weeks collecting firewood to build the Holi, just as young people do in England for the Guy Fawkes bonfire.

It was a wonderful experience to set the Holi alight. The fragrance of sweet-smelling oils and incense that were used was carried far and wide along the sea shore. Children took the opportunity of roasting corn in the fire. It was felt that corn roasted in the Holi would cure toothache.

Diwali was a less colourful affair than it is today. Candles were expensive and not so common. Traditional diyas and apinyas gave way to solitary oil lamps.

Cheddi Attends Secondary School

Cheddi attended the R.N. Persaud High School at Port Mourant for his secondary education. It was a very big step for the family and the decision to send him there was only made after the matter had been discussed at length with Headmaster Ralph.

Secondary education was as yet not free, this meant that school fees had to be paid. He had to be better turned-out and had to wear shoes - at least while on school premises. The cost of this decision and the sacrifices made by his family left a deep impression on young Cheddi and were to influence a major part of his adult life.

If the decision to attend High School was a big one, an even more important decision was the one to send him to the country's premier school, Queen's College, in the capital city of Georgetown. In Cheddi's own words, at Port Mourant he was 'a big fish in a small pond'.

CHAPTER 8
HELLO GEORGETOWN!

Queen's College

Queen's College was founded in 1844 to educate the children of Europeans. In time it began to admit pupils one of whose parents were Europeans. Much later, other groups were admitted.

The name given to those coming from the rural areas was 'country-booboo'. Most of the parents whose children attended the college were merchants, doctors, lawyers or civil servants.

The accent with which Cheddi spoke would have been different from that of the children from Georgetown. Indeed, he required a great amount of self-confidence and brashness to overcome the teasing he got.

As he was so badly treated by the families with whom he stayed, it took him quite a long time to get used to city life. Much depended on how quickly he could make friends. Cheddi was good at cricket and this helped.

Although his parents were paying for his board and lodging the first family he stayed with expected him to perform such household chores as washing their car and cutting grass for the goat . To do such chores in Port Mourant was one thing, but for a Queen's College boy to be seen doing them was an added cause of teasing from the other pupils.

At Port Mourant there was little social difference

among Indians. Indentureship had helped to reduce the influence of caste, while in the city, a person's position in society and money helped the caste system to re-emerge and flourish.

The Jagans were believed to be from the lower caste of the Kurmi. On the other hand the second family in Georgetown with whom he stayed were of the higher, Kshatriya caste. He was forced to sleep on the floor although there was a spare room with a bed in the house. He was also sent on errands to the market. What made matters worse was that the family had three boys who also attended Queen's College and they were neither expected nor asked to do such tasks.

The third family had converted to the Catholic religion and it was with them that he at last felt really comfortable.

Georgetown

Unlike Port Mourant, Georgetown had a lot to offer. At college firm friendships are made and in Cheddi's case, Orrin Dummett was to remain a life-long friend. They shared much with each other, such as rides along the sea wall and on Sunday afternoons, they went to the Botanic Gardens to feed the manatees. There was also the cinema on Saturday mornings or the one-thirty matinee..

Films such as Fu Manchu and Captain Marvel were city delights comparable to fishing for patwa or hourie at Port Mourant.

Cheddi, already capable of holding his own on the cricket pitch with a bat made from coconut branches and using seeds for a ball, did not take long to prove himself with a proper bat, ball and pads.

In time the school record books showed proof of his ability as a member of the third eleven cricket team.After two years at Queen's, Cheddi returned home to Port Mourant having passed both the Oxford and Cambridge Lower and School Certificate examinations.

Feeding A Manatee In The Botanic Gardens, Georgetown

Stabroek Market, Georgetown

CHAPTER 9
RETURN TO PORT MOURANT

It is 1935 and Cheddi is now seventeen years old. He has spent three years in the city, attended the best college in the country, mixed with different peoples and seen more things and places than any other child on the estate.

The bicycle and spinning top he has brought with him, the first on the estate, are the envy of all the other boys and girls.

Whatever impact Georgetown and Queen's College may have had on him, Cheddi returned to Port Mourant 'unscathed'. The folks in Georgetown had not succeeded in citifying him with their Creole, middle-class Christian ways. For him it was life as usual or was it?

But influence him in some way they did, as could be seen when Cheddi adopted the middle name, Berret. Indeed the influence was so difficult to avoid that even his younger brothers and sisters were given the names, Derek, Doris, Patricia and Barbara. This meant that the Indian tradition of naming babies after rivers, gods, goddesses, heroes, heroines, flowers and seasons was sacrificed under the Christian influence. On more important matters however, the strength of Hindu culture and tradition held firm.

Neither his parents nor Cheddi himself were in favour of his becoming a Christian so as to be considered for a job as a teacher. It was one thing adopting a Christian first name, quite another giving-up one's religion.

At seventeen years of age what were Cheddi's options in looking for a job? To obtain a job as a pupil teacher he would have to become a Christian and that was out of the question.

What of the Civil Service? Although it was open to few East Indians, much more depended on the applicant's background and social contacts than on a High School Certificate. After several attempts it became evident that a job in the Civil Service was closed to him.

What of a job in the Port Mourant estate office as a clerk, trainee bookkeeper or in the estate's distillery? Such jobs were regarded as dead-end and the prospect of their eldest son ending up with a job on the estate was enough to urge his parents to redouble their efforts to help him escape.

Whilst waiting for a decision to be made, Cheddi was apprenticed to a tailor.

What of Cheddi in all this one might ask? What did he want to do about his future? As a young boy he was impressed by Dr. Kennard, the medical officer for the district who called at the Jagan's home when someone was ill. Could he become a medical doctor?

'Send The Boy To Study'

When asked for his advice,Dr. J.B. Singh, then a member of the Legislative Council or Parliament and a friend of the family, replied: 'Jagan, why waste the boy's time? Don't worry with the Civil Service. Send the boy to study.'

This was of course easier said than done. The big question was where was the money to come from? It was all right for Dr. Singh to suggest such a thing, for his family had land and several head of cattle.The Jagans had little.

However, the idea, once planted could not be put to rest so easily.

Two matters had to be settled. The cost and what to study? Law was considered. But this meant going to England and studying full-time while his parents financed his up-keep. Since the Jagans could not afford this, the idea was quickly dismissed.

In addition, Cheddi associated law with being a good speaker and at eighteen years old, he had not yet mastered that art.

The United States of America offered just the right opportunity for working and studying. His friend, Orrin, had enrolled to study dentistry at Howard University. The fees were low; so dentistry it was.

Scraping together all the money the Jagans could lay their hands on, $500 in local currency then worth about £100, Cheddi, with the blessings and tears of his parents, brothers and sisters, set sail in 1936 with his college mate and friend, Orrin, for Boston.

Cheddi Sets Sail For America

Cheddi left a Guyana where history, if it existed at all was a record of somebody else's past, texts one read in books.

Without his knowing it, on the very ship in which he sailed, the black crew members were segregated from their white mates.

The first port of call, Boston, was the home of the legendary Boston Tea Pary, where in 1773 colonists boarded ships, owned by Britain and dumped their cargoes of tea overboard. In doing so, they were refusing to pay a tax imposed by the British government. 'No Taxation Without Representation' may not have been invented by the Bostonians but it triggered eight years of the War of Independence (1775-1783) and the founding of the present day United States of America.

Cheddi may also not have been aware of the activities of the Ku Klux Klan. These were men with fiery crosses, whips and bombs, who struck terror into the lives of black people. Nor would he have heard while attending Queen's College of a Jamaican by the name of Marcus Garvey who organised the fight back against the Klan.

Nothing in his eighteen years could have prepared him for these aspects of life in the United States of America.

CHAPTER 10
SOJOURN IN THE UNITED STATES OF AMERICA

Howard University, where Cheddi spent his first two years, was founded in 1867. It was named after a graduate of West Point who was a Union Officer during the American Civil War. Although the university was founded for the education of black people, it did open its doors to all races.

At Howard the two year course offered him a good start to his seven-year American sojourn. The fees were low and it was one of the best universities in the country.

Like Port Mourant, a university town or campus could be very sheltered. Meals, lodgings and books are often provided on site. In Cheddi's case, he and Orrin shared a room off the campus. This was not difficult because the university, although situated in spacious and beautiful grounds, was in the middle of the city's black community.

First Snow Flakes and Missing Home

Even the winters did not bother him. Like most visitors from the tropics he was very excited when he saw the first snow-flakes, although he found spending his first Christmas away from his own relatives a sad affair. Most students on campus went to their own relatives. No one invited him to spend Christmas with them as would have been the case in Guyana where anyone away from their loved ones at Christmas would have been invited to people's homes for the festivities.

At Howard as at Queen's, the course he was doing did not prepare him much for the world outside. Social Science subjects were excluded from the course.

If he passed his exams with excellent grades then he would win a scholarship. This he succeeded in doing - a free place during his second year at Howard and entry into the Northwestern University Dental School in Chicago.

Chicago: The City That Moulded Him

Cheddi spent five years in the city and it was to be as important as his home, Port Mourant, in moulding his future years.

His formal education was almost complete and by 1942 he had gained his second degree, in Dental Surgery. His first was a Bachelor of Science degree.

However, it was the education he received just by living and working in the city, as well as the interest he took in events that were unfolding in India and Europe which helped influence his views.

Cheddi's first shock occurred when it was not possible for him to share lodgings with his friend, Orrin, as they had done at Howard University. Although he was able to secure a room near to the university, the north side of Chicago was out of bounds to blacks. Cheddi was only able to live there because students from India, Japan and Hawaii were not regarded as black.The university in which he was studying, liberal though it was, operated a quota system on enrolling blacks and Jews.

On his travels in America, Cheddi learnt at first-hand what racial segregation was all about. Once, while travelling to East Virginia from Columbia with a black friend, he was told that because of the jim crow law his friend would have to sit at the back of the coach once they had crossed the state boundary. Cheddi chose to remain at the back with his friend.

Matters were no different when it came to hotel rooms and he refused to stay in one after he learnt that he was able to obtain a room without a reservation, while an African girl was not allowed to stay there, even though her room had been booked in advance.

Cheddi saw for himself the American version of the caste system. Asians were not regarded as black and were therefore afforded the status of honorary whites.

Working and Studying

Like many students whose parents were not able to maintain them at university, Cheddi was forced to do a variety of part-time jobs including those of dish-washer, elevator-operator, presser and salesman. At one time he even managed to do three jobs together, those of salesman, newspaper deliverer and ice cream vendor.

The tailoring skills which he had learnt at home helped

him to get work in a pawnshop repairing and mending articles of clothing.

There were of course many jobs that, with experience, one tried to avoid, jobs such as being a presser in a laundry during the summer. American summers can be very hot and oppressive.

On the other hand, a night job as an elevator-operator offered a good chance during the long night shift to catch up on one's studies.

Education Of A Different Kind

The scene was quite different away from the campus, among the working people. So different, that a new word had to be coined to describe the period. This was the Depression during which millions were unemployed. To assist people to get back to work, President Roosevelt introduced the New Deal.

This was a programme developed to assist industry and promote public-works projects so as to revive the economy.

Far away in Europe, that continent was at war fighting fascism. Very soon the United States was to join the fighting, supporting France, Russia, China, Britain and other countries which comprised the British Commonwealth of nations.

Despite the effects of the Depression, Chicago, the centre of the beef, wheat and railroad industries, seemed like a haven compared with Europe and all the fighting

Dr Cheddi Jagan, Shri Jawaharlal Nehru and Mr Forbes Burnham in New Delhi in 1953

that was taking place there. Cheddi was able to observe the effects of the Depression on clerks, small shop keepers and those who had migrated to the city to share in the boom years of the previous decade.

He would stop to listen to the speeches at Bughouse Square, near the Clarke Street slum, a sort of Speakers' Corner in Chicago. He left these meetings full of inspiration .

The Jig Saw Puzzle Not Yet Complete

While studying at Northwestern University, Cheddi was able to meet and mix with students from many parts of the world. Sometimes, late into the night their discussions would range from religion, politics and economics to cricket. Cheddi was aware that his primary and secondary schools at Port Mourant, Georgetown and then at Howard, had not helped to broaden the base of his education.

Never one to refuse a challenge, he enrolled for classes at the local YMCA, studying economics, sociology and politics. While there, he met Professor Sinha, a lecturer. Professor Sinha, an exile, kept the students informed about events in India. There, thousands were taking part in civil campaigns aimed at forcing the British government to grant independence. As a result, many of the demonstrators were imprisoned.

The story of one of India's foremost fighters for independence, Jawaharlal Nehru, as told in his book,Towards Freedom , made a great impression on Cheddi.

Had Cheddi studied in England, the influences on him might have been different. As it was, the United States own War of Independence from Britain in 1776, The American Constitution, Roosevelt's New Deal Programme, and the book, Robber Barons , by Matthew Josephson were the main ideas which influenced him.

At last, rather like a jig saw puzzle, the pieces began to come together. His parents' poverty, manager Gibson's mansion set alongside the hovels in which many lived, the victims of the Depression, the war against fascism, India's fight for freedom and racial discrimination, all made him realise what he must fight for: freedom for India today and for his own Guyana tomorrow. A spark had been lit.

Cheddi Considers Joining The American Army

Life in America was not made up only of studying. It was whilst at a students' party that Cheddi met Janet Rosenberg, his future wife.

The summer months which he spent in New York brought back memories of the Caribbean and what better way to spend leisure time out of doors than in a game of cricket?

The winters in the United States are very severe. These, together with long hours at work and study eventually took their toll on Cheddi. In the winter of 1942, he had to go to hospital where he was X-rayed and a small speck was found on his left lung. On further examination he was diagnosed as suffering from tuberculosis

(TB).

Fortunately, rest and time spent in a sanatorium were enough to cure the illness and by the spring of 1943 he was back on his feet and looking for work. Although he had qualified as a dentist the previous year he was unable to work in that field.

Before he was allowed to practise, it was necessary for him to obtain a certificate from the State Examination Board. Only United States citizens could sit such an examination.

While not prepared to offer him citizenship, the United States laws did however permit him to join the army to defend the country - but only as a private, not as an officer.

Why, you may ask would Cheddi, recently qualified as a dentist, want to sacrifice his life for the United States of America? Many Guyanese, West Indians and millions of others like Cheddi did in fact view the war as a just fight against fascist regimes.

It was felt that a victory for fascism would have made it more difficult to achieve independence for their own countries.

On 7 December 1941, Japan bombed Pearl Harbour, a port in Hawaii , one of the States which makes up the United States. This action so enraged Americans that they joined the war against fascism.

Marriage

In 1943 Cheddi married Janet. As she was an American citizen, marriage to her would have entitled him to become a United States citizen and to take the State Board examination. Instead he and Janet decided to make their home in Guyana.

CHAPTER 11
RETURN TO GUYANA

Cheddi, now a qualified dentist, twenty-six years old, was a changed person to the eighteen-year old who had left the shores of Guyana eight years before.

He was a much more aware and confident person, in readiness for the struggles before him. As a qualified dentist he had an independent means of earning a living. He did not have to work for the government. But, what of the country and its people?

Reform is Overdue

In Guyana, the Second World War (1939-1945) had the effect of postponing many internal reforms which were now long-overdue. Some of these reforms - apart from the most important,which was the need to change the Constitution - included dealing with the pressure for higher wages to meet rising prices. The British government of Guyana had not changed since 1928.

Of the two most dramatic changes in the country, one was the presence of troops from the United States of America .The result of a Lend-Lease Agreement between President Roosevelt and Prime Minister Churchill for the British government.

The other was that the size of the country had been reduced - the result of another agreement between Britain and Brazil. In both cases the people of Guyana were not consulted.

The sugar industry continued to have a great influence on the policies of the government despite the fact that the economy had begun to change. Other products such as rice, timber, gold and bauxite were making a contribution to the revenue of the country. However the interests of this sector, especially that of rice, were not taken much into account.

Many professionals like Dr. Jagan had returned from abroad and had been active in the Trade Union Movement and other political and social groups, membership of which had been increasing greatly. People in the rural areas and particularly those living on or near sugar estates suffered as much as those in the towns from the policies pursued by the sugar barons.

The question was, how to channel this dissatisfaction along positive lines.

Looking For Answers

Cheddi however had a few everyday matters to sort out. Preparations had to be made to receive his young bride. Premises for his surgery had to be found. As the eldest son in a family which now consisted of five sisters and five brothers, he was expected to assist them. To add to these matters he was almost a stranger to the city of Georgetown where he had spent his student days.

His spare time was spent playing bridge and cricket. As a member of the East Indian Association, he was a regular contributor to its newspaper, Indian Opinion. He later became treasurer of the Man-Power Citizens' Association (MPCA) at that time the leading Trade Union representing workers in the Sugar Industry. Both organisations failed to satisfy his yearning to be of service to his country.

As a stranger to Georgetown and to the country's social and political life, Cheddi had to continue his search for a framework within which to place what he made of both the American and Guyanese radical traditions.

Part of the answer was to be found in the books of Marx and Lenin. The message was threefold. First, workers produced the wealth of the world and most of the wealth was creamed off by the people of capital - capitalists.

Secondly that deep social change occurs because of different classes of people in society wanting to bring about change.

Thirdly, that all the workers of the world had much in common and should unite.

Cheddi Enters Politics

Cheddi became a member of a discussion circle at the Carnegie Library in Georgetown, he wrote letters to the Press on topical issues and in other ways helped widen the level of contact between different groups of people. All this activity eventually led in 1946, to the formation with others of the Political Affairs Committee (PAC).

The founding members of the Committee were Janet and Cheddi Jagan, Ashton Chase and Jocelyn Hubbard - they were active trades unionists. The Committee published and circulated a Bulletin .

That same year, 1946, also saw the birth of the Women's Political and Economic Organisation (WPEO), the leading figures of which were, Janet Jagan, Frances Stafford and Winifred Gaskin. The founding of this organisation, the first of its kind in the country, made it possible for women to play a part in wider issues affecting them - such as nursery education for their children, better facilities for market huskers and the right to vote at twenty-one.

Shooting Of Workers At Enmore Estate

Three years of activity among sugar-workers, rural peasants and the city folk brought results with his election in 1947 as the youngest member of the Legislative Council - the body which made the laws of the country.

Within a year of Dr Jagans' victory at the polls the bitter-sweet taste of sugar was to be felt. The scene was on one of the estates,Enmore, the actors were the workers, the sugar planters and the government.

The end of the Second World War in 1945 resulted in a drop in the demand for sugar. The sugar planters in an attempt to reduce the bill for wages while at the same time increase production, sought to change the working conditions.

The workers on eight estates along the coast in the county of Demerara opposed the changes and staged one of the longest strikes in the history of the industry. For four months, the estates were shut down. Many families were at the point of starvation but it was felt that if the employers were allowed to introduce the changes it would bring more harm than good.

On June 16, 1948, the police opened fire, shot and killed five and injured several more workers.

The shooting shocked the country. This incident was to affect Dr. Jagan so very deeply (he knew personally many of those killed) that he secretly pledged, 'there was to be no turning back' , he would fight for justice and bread for his people to the end.

Janet Jagan

CHAPTER 12
JANET JAGAN

The important role played by women as mothers, wives, friends, secretaries and comrades has only recently been receiving the attention which it deserves. For Janet, Cheddi's wife and comrade these past fifty years, the reverse may be true.

A scapegoat is a person who is made to bear the blame for others; well that is what has been her lot, especially during the 1950s and 1960s when matters were going badly for the Party and the country. For months she could not go to the cinema, the market, the shops or even be seen in public on her own.

Born into a Jewish family which migrated from Eastern Europe to the United States during the last century, she knows what it is like to be an outsider.

Like many young people during the 1940s, Janet wanted to join the American army so as to fight the war against fascism. She decided to train as a nurse. Both Cheddi and Janet wanted to enlist in the armed forces.

Janet Arrives in Guyana

However, that was not to be. Within a year of their marriage she was on her way to Guyana to join her husband and to start a new life. Arriving in Georgetown, where, like Cheddi, she was a stranger, she found it difficult to settle-in despite the proverbial hospitality for which the

Guyanese are well known.

It was not at all easy for Janet to get accustomed to such things as the water supply, the food, mosquitoes and sandflies and Georgetown social life with its many taboos.

When Cheddi's parents received the news that he had married a white American, they were shocked and disappointed. As Hindus they expected their son to marry a Hindu . Janet felt that they must have missed the fuss and ceremony of a Hindu wedding for their eldest son.

The white people with whom the family had contact were mainly estate overseers - the relationship being one of master and servant. The one other European with whom they had some contact and who treated them with respect was Dr. Kennard who was a general medical practitioner on the Corentyne.

To Pre-judge is To Be Prejudiced

What were Cheddi's parents expecting of this stranger - their Boujee or daughter-in-law who was now in their midst, and who would be sharing their humble home? Whatever the feelings of individual members of the family may have been, the old tradition of hospitality that was bred into all Hindus and Guyanese won out in the end.

They were pleasantly surprised when they realised that her sympathies were with the working people. They were also grateful to her for the support she gave to Cheddi in taking on the education of his brothers and sisters. This is how Cheddi's father summed it up. 'If Cheddi bin marry a coolie gal, me pickney (child) would a never get a chance.' ('If Cheddi had married a Hindu girl, she might not have been happy for Cheddi to spend his money on educating his own brothers and sisters.')

Some members of the Jagan family may have judged Janet before getting to know her as a person - to pre-judge is to be prejudiced.

The greatest shock of all was her visit to her in-law's home at Port Mourant. It was a very simple household. As Janet recalls of her first meeting with Mr. and Mrs Jagan, 'They did not know what to do with me'. Should she sit with the men or be with the women in the kitchen, as was the custom?

With the birth of their son, Cheddi Junior, and later their daughter, Indira, Janet had to cope with being a mother, dental assistant and hygienist as well as, much later, a political activist.

Janet Enters Politics

A founder member of the Political Affairs Committee, Janet later helped found the Women's Political and Economic Organisation (WPEO) together with Winifred Gaskin and Frances Stafford. She was later elected Secretary to the Clerical Workers' Union.

Her decision to contest the general elections in 1947 changed the mood and atmosphere of the contest. Although she was a popular candidate she lost to John Fernandes. In the General Election of 1953 under universal adult suffrage, she was elected to the House of Assembly and has served as a Minister of Health and Home Affairs.

Janet Imprisoned

She was sentenced to a term of imprisonment with hard labour in 1955 after having been convicted of possessing a Secret Police Manual and for holding a public meeting without the permission of the police.

Over the years, she has been both General Secretary of the People's Progressive Party and editor of the Party's newspaper, Thunder and later the Mirror - a job which she continues to enjoy and which took her away from the limelight.

Today, whilst she is still active in the Party's civic functions and on state occasions, Janet enjoys writing stories in the folk tradition of her adopted country. She first told many of these stories to her grandchildren and they were later published in the Mirror.

In 1993 on the occasion of the seventeenth Anniversary of Independence, Janet was awarded the Order of Excellence 'for her selfless role, her unflagging commitment and the eminence and distinction achieved by her struggle for the independence of Guyana and, more recently, in the restoration of democracy.'

Without Janet's devotion and support as wife, mother

and comrade of Cheddi it would have been much more difficult and perhaps impossible for him to have made such a profound contribution.

Janet is the author of 'When Granpa Cheddi was a boy and other stories' a collection based on the stories she told to her grandchildren . The book is published by Peepal Tree Press. A second collection is due out later.

Dr. and Mrs. Cheddi Jagan *Mr. L. F. S. Burham*
Three Founding Members of the PPP

CHAPTER 13
THE 1953 ELECTIONS

The General Elections held in 1953 were different from any other held before or since. They were the first to be held under the new Constitution and universal adult suffrage.

For the first time, all adults over the age of twenty-one were entitled to vote. Also for the first time, political parties winning a majority of seats were expected to form a government. This meant that political parties had come to stay. The role of independent candidates seeking the support of the electorate in a particular constituency became a thing of the past.

Hundreds of voters supported the political party of their choice instead of as in the past because of the race and ethnic origin of the candidate with the result that the two main racial groups - Africans and East Indians - were united.

The People's Progressive Party (P.P.P) founded by members of the PAC in 1950, now included in its leadership, L.F.S Burnham, a prominent lawyer and Trade Unionist as its chairman . Among others included Ashton Chase,Ivan Edwards,Ivan Cendrecourt, B. Blackman, all trade unionists, Eusi Kwayana and Martin Carter.

The P.P.P was the first modern political party to be formed in the country.The Party campainged for the new system of voting and the new constitution which was introduced. During the day, the Jagans' dental surgery in Charlotte Street, Georgetown ,served as headquarters of the campaign as well as a surgery. The party newspaper,Thunder, then a monthly had to be produced, manifestos and other literature distributed, public meetings organised - all this had to be done while the business of the surgery was being conducted. Hundreds of people, both young and old were caught up in the general excitement of the movement for freedom. They sold newspapers, raised funds, spoke at and attended public meetings.

Street corner meetings became popular events. Senior citizens carrying stools to sit on arrived early to hear their favourite speakers.

The newspapers, radio and the Church also became actively involved in politics and played a great part in educating voters as to which political party they should vote for and why. The media and the Church were not neutral and advised voters which party to support . In the main they did not support the People's Progressive Party.

The PPP Manifesto

In supporting the People's Progressive Party, voters had the opportunity of supporting the programme or manifesto of that party. Some of the main points of the manifesto may today be taken for granted. However, during the 1950's, such demands were considered by many people to be too radical or impossible to achieve.

The Manifesto advocated:

1. Self-government under universal adult suffrage and a voting age of 18.
2. A living wage for all.
3. Free and compulsory education for all.
   A greater say for civic groups in the administration and content of subjects that were taught in schools.
4. The right of workers to choose the trade union they wished to represent them.
5. A minimum wage for all.
6. Reform of the tax laws in favour of the less well-off.
7. Removal of the ban which prevented other leaders from the West Indies visiting Guyana.
8. Removal of the ban on importing literature.

Victory At Last

It was as though everyone sensed that great changes were around the corner and that it was important to influence those changes.

With the media and the Church against them, the People's Progressive Party led by Dr. Jagan was accused of wanting to ban religious worship, of planning to take away people's land and to take control of the schools. Members of the Party, lacking the resources of the other parties were prevented from speaking on the radio but relied on a committed band of workers to spread their message.

With the election results declared, the Party won a landslide victory, taking eighteen of the twenty-four seats in the Assembly, the new name for the Council which made the laws of the country. However, the Opposition was not satisfied with the results and with the support of the British and American governments, continued to harass the Party in office and plot to bring about its downfall.

CHAPTER 14
ONE HUNDRED AND THIRTY-THREE DAYS LATER

During the short period that the Party was in office, it passed laws removing the ban on people and books entering the country, provided more protection for rice farmers and required employers to negotiate with trade unions which enjoyed the majority support of their members.The government also awarded more scholarships to enable children from poorer families to receive free secondary education.

After one hundred and thirty-three days of being in office, the British government suspended the Constitution on October 9, 1953. The Party was dismissed from office. Troops were sent from England to enforce new laws called the 'Emergency Regulations'.To justify its actions, the British government accused the People's Progressive Party of 'wanting to set up a communist dictatorship.'

The action taken by the British government came as a shock to people in Guyana. For many, it was the first time they had seen British troops with armoured vehicles on their soil . However, the people heeded the Partys' advice and remained calm.

The suspension of the Constitution was followed by months of terror during which meetings, books and newspapers were banned. Houses were ransacked during the wee hours of the morning. People were detained without trial and normal civil liberties were suspended.

One of the books banned was a collection of poetry, Poems of Resistance by Martin Carter,who was also detained without trial along with, Adjodha Singh, Sydney King (now known as Eusi Kwayana), Balli Latchmansingh, Rory Westmass and George Bowman. Many Party members were imprisoned for travelling to see their loved ones or their constituents.

Such laws were a denial of Dr. Jagan's human rights. He broke the order which restricted him from leaving the city of Georgetown and was sentenced to six months' imprisonment with hard labour.

Even his opponents were shocked at the decision of the magistrate and considered the sentence much too harsh.

For Dr. Jagan, however, a term of imprisonment was a price he felt it necessary to pay during Guyana's struggle for independence. Two patriots of India, Mahatma Gandhi and Jaharwalal Nehru had both done so before him.

The Party Splits

One of the effects of the actions of the British government in suspending the Constitution was to cause a split in the People's Progressive Party. Mr. L.F.S. Burnham, the Chairman of the Party, together with some supporters broke away from the main Party. For some time, the two parties existed side by side, both claiming to be the genuine People's Progressive Party

The ending of the partnership between Mr. Burnham and Dr. Jagan was deeply regretted by the vast majority of the population. The partnership was seen as the means of uniting Guyana's two major communities, and of putting aside cultural and communal differences for the good of the country in its struggle for independence from Britain. Many believed that both would be re-united at some future date, but such hopes proved false. Eventually, the faction led by Mr. Burnham re-named itself, the People's National Congress.

Having helped to split the national movement, the British government felt it safe to set a date for the next general election.

Civil Unrest

Once again, the People's Progressive Party won a majority of seats in the general elections held in 1957. This victory at the polls was again repeated in 1961. So, for the third time the Party led by Dr. Jagan had won at the polls despite the fact that it had lost many of its most prominent members.

However, the Opposition never accepted the results of the polls and continued to harry the government. As a result, the party was unable to govern properly during the next four years and the country was torn by strikes, arson attacks and general civil unrest.

Never before had Guyana gone through such experiences and, it is hoped that it will never again have to do so. Friends and neighbours who had grown up with each other were torn apart. Children and young people as well as adults took sides and very often people acted out their prejudices by attacking each other.

Proportional Representation

A new election was held in 1964 under the system of Proportional Representation.The new system of voting was most unusual for a British colony. Most of Britain's colonies' Constitutions had been modelled on the first past the post system - like that of elections to the House of Commons. It was felt that the British government made the change so as to please the Opposition parties in Guyana and to bring about the defeat of the People's Progressive Party.

Despite this change, Dr. Jagan and the People's Progressive Party were returned with a majority of seats. However the Party was not chosen to form a government. The opposition, the People's National Congress and its allies were chosen.

For the following twenty-eight years, Dr. Jagan was Leader of the Opposition in the House of Assembly. For most people to have spent such a long time out of office would have been enough to make them abandon the political stage altogether. Indeed this is what many advised him to do. However, he was not to be put off and continued the struggle for independence which was achieved in 1976.

Although Guyana won independence from Britain, this did not bring full democracy and the Party had to carry on the fight for free and fair elections.

In the elections held on October 1992, the Party was returned to office, this time with the blessing and help of both the British and American governments. Dr. Jagan was elected President of the Republic of Guyana.

Dr Jagan when he was leader of the opposition

CHAPTER 15
FATHER OF MODERN POLITICS

When Britain made Guyana a Crown Colony in 1927, it set back the development of the country many years.

By the 1950s, there was much pent-up anger and frustration. One of the main reasons for this was that not many people were eligible to vote. The Voters' List was compiled on the basis of the income that a person earned and on the property they owned. The result was that the majority did not participate in electing their representatives who in turn made laws which governed everyone.

Elected members of the country's Parliament were independents and not subject to any Party rules. Those elected, represented their districts and were only seen during elections. The arrival of the Jagans was to change all this.

Although he was elected as an independent member in 1947, the youngest at twenty-nine, Dr. Jagan very soon emerged as the most consistent lone voice in the Council, speaking on behalf of and defending the rights and interests of all the working people and not just of those from his own district. Dr. Jagan was able to do so by exposing what was taking place in the Council to the people at street corner meetings throughout the year and not just at election times.

A political meeting held under a silk cotton tree

Dr. Jagan - A Speaker and Author

Success as a political figure owes as much to one's personality and ability to communicate as to knowledge of the subject. Dr. Jagan was to excel in all three areas. His winning personality persuaded many people to become members of and help to build the oldest Party in the country.

His ability to communicate was not restricted to street corner meetings and other large open air gatherings. In 1952 he spoke for six hours in the Legislative Council Chamber in an effort to prevent the passage of a Bill to ban books.

During Dr. Jagan's early membership of the Council, he soon realised that it was simply not enough to make speeches but that it was necessary for him to study all the documents put out by the government and other sources so that when he rose to speak, he knew the subject and was prepared.

Dr. Jagan was also concerned that people outside must have a chance to know what was taking place in the various departments of government. Of all the rights enshrined in the United Nations Charter, the freedom of information and the right to publish were recognised very early by him and acted upon.

From the early days of the Bulletin to those of the party organ,Thunder, later The Mirror, Dr. Jagan has established a long tradition in this field. unlike other leaders in the West Indies..

Bitter Sugar

This is the title of one of Dr. Jagan's most well-known publications. How, one might ask could sugar be bitter? So powerful has the sugar industry been in the history of the country that for many, Booker's Guyana (BG) was often used in place of British Guyana - Booker's being the main sugar producers and employers in the country.

Dr. Jagan was able to show that throughout its history, the sugar industry and later Booker's did all they could to prevent other industries from developing. Through their ownership of shares in newspapers, radio, the retail and wholesale trades and shipping.

Booker's the largest employer of labour, was able not only to keep wages low but also to influence policies made by the government.

The result was that working people paid a very heavy price as a sugar producing country in terms of poor housing, land-hungry peasantry, poor drainage and irrigation and government by civil servants from London.

Roving Ambassador For Guyana's Freedom

Although Guyana is situated on the South American mainland there have always been strong ties and links with the Islands in the West Indies.

From the beginning, Dr. Jagan has sought to develop and strengthen these ties by personal visits and contacts despite the actions of the St. Vincent government in seizing his passport and declaring Mrs Jagan a prohibited immigrant in 1949.

While other leaders would choose to spend their holidays in the United States of America or in Europe, he very often chose the West Indies. In this way beginning in 1945, on a visit to Trinidad for the first time, he was able to meet with other leading figures in the region while at the same time enjoying a holiday.

After 1947, he was able to travel and speak as a Member of the Legislative Council. By 1950 he had visited all the major islands including the Dominican Republic, Curacao and Haiti.

Dr. Jagan Visits London

In 1951 he paid his first of many visits to London where he held discussions with the then Colonial Office and spoke at meetings organised by West Indians living in Britain.

He met with Colonial Office civil servants and urged upon them the need for reform and independence for Guyana. By 1953 Dr. Jagan had already begun to be recognised as the leading political figure in Guyana and indeed the West Indies.After the government was dismissed in October 1953, both he and Mr. Burnham travelled to London and India to put the case for Guyana's freedom before the world's Press.

Dr. Jagan, as Leader of the Opposition, was ceaseless in promoting the cause of freedom and justice for the people of Guyana. These efforts have taken him to many capital cities of the world, attending Trades Unions Congresses, peace meetings and other conferences.

In a career spanning five generations, his influence on the political and social scene in the West Indies is immense. He is one of the longest serving members of any legislature in the world. As a West Indian whose forefathers came from India, he is the first to be elected to the highest office in the region.

Today, aged seventy-six, his life and times are far from complete, whilst his contribution to the triumph of democracy in Guyana is unlikely to be challenged.

Dr Jagan has received many awards for his services to and solidarity with the International Working Class movement. .

Highlights in Cheddi Jagan's Career

22.3.1918	Birth of Cheddi
1924-1933	Attended schools at Port Mourant and Rosehall
1933-1935	Student at Queen's College, Georgetown
1936	Sets sail for the United States of America
1942	Qualifies as a Dental Surgeon
1943	Marries Janet Rosenberg
1943	Returns home
1946	Formation of the Political Affairs Committee
1947-53	Elected the youngest member of the Legislative Council
1948	Enmore shooting and Jagan re-dedicates himself to working for his people's freedom
1950	People's Progressive Party (PPP) - first Party Congress
1951	Visits the United Kingdom for the first time
1953	The People's Progressive Party wins a majority of seats in the House of Assembly with Dr. Jagan as Chief Minister
1953	The PPP is dismissed from office
1953.	Dr. Jagan and L.F.S. Burnham, the Party's chairman visits the United King-

	dom and India to put the case for Guyana's freedom before the world's press
April 1954	Sentenced to six months imprisonment with hard labour
Sept. 1954	Janet Jagan sent to prison for six months
1957-64	The PPP wins a majority of seats at the General Elections and forms a government
1964-92	Leader of the Opposition
1992	Elected President of the Republic of Guyana

Books written by Dr Jagan include::

The West on Trial -The Fight for Guyana 's Freedom .

A new edition is now available from Hansib Publications. London.

POSTSCRIPT
Indentureship
Phase 1
Terms and Conditions

Today, trades unions and employers agree on a contract of employment which is binding on both parties. Under indentureship, the conditions were set by the employers. It was a one-way contract.

During the seventy-nine years indentureship of labour from India was in force, the system went through many phases. Whatever changes were made over the years the intention remained the same. To provide the estates with a plentiful supply of cheap labour.

Conditions were so bad that the Governor of Guyana was forced to look into the matter.

What the contract did provide was:

Hours of work:

From six in the morning to six in the evening.The time it took to get to work was not included and a walk of three to five miles was not unusual.Boys under fourteen and children were not under contract.

A weekly allowance of :

13 lbs of rice
11/2lb of salted fish
3/4lb of onions

A brass cup to serve four person

A small quantity of salt, pepper, ghee or oil and tamarind.

Wages were Fixed for the period [duration] of the contract

Clothing - issued once every Year

Two blankets

A jacket

Loin cloth of four and a half yards of cloth

A cap

A wooden bowl

A brass cup to serve four people

At the end of the contract immigrants could choose to return to India free of charge. Of the 396 who arrived in 1838, only sixty chose to remain.

Indentureship
Phase 2

For six years no immigrants arrived from India. Although 17,000 did arrive from Madeira, Hong Kong and Africa. As a result of discussions between India, the British government and the owners of estates, the trade was resumed in 1851. One of the new conditions was that the expenses of the trade were to be met by the taxpayer in British Guyana.

For the next twenty years the relationship between employer and employee was like that of master and servant:

> Workers were not allowed to give evidence in court on their own behalf.
>
> Those workers wishing to leave their place of work were required to carry passes and police were posted at certain points to enforce the law.
>
> It was not uncommon for magistrates to impose a fine of two days' wages for each day's absence from work. Many workers served their sentences either in jail or working on the estates.

The welfare of all people on contract was under the control of a civil servant and the Immigration Agent-General, James Crosby who was the longest serving official to hold the post - from 1858 to 1880, he became a friend of the immigrant and for many years after his death the position he held came to be known by his name.

Phase 3 (Or The De Voeux Phase)

It is often the case that tragedies help to speed up change. In 1869, workers went on strike and were shot and killed at Plantation Leonora. The killing led to an increase in public concern and to the appointment of another Commission of Enquiry in 1870. The report of the Commission became known as the De Voeux Report.

Some of the changes introduced as a result of the report included:

> allowing workers to give evidence on their own behalf in court;
>
> those workers who had completed their tasks for the day were free to leave the estate
>
> and
>
> workers were no longer imprisoned for refusing to work - fines were imposed instead.

Despite these welcome changes, the powers previously granted to officials like Crosby to look into the welfare of immigrants were gradually withdrawn due to pressure from estate owners.

QUESTIONS

1. List four qualities in Cheddi Jagan which you most admire and give reasons for your choice.

2. Which public figure do you most admire? Give reasons for your choice.

3. Dr. Jagan became a dentist almost by accident. What type work would you like to do? Give reasons for your choice.

4. Bwoy awee proppa suffa' do you think this still applies today? Give reasons for your answers.

5. Can you compare life on a sugar estate today, in contrast to Cheddi's childhood days spent on Port Mourant sugar estate?

6a. If you were to migrate to another country, which one would you choose? Give your reasons for wanting to go there.

6b. If your parents/guardians have migrated, ask them their reasons for doing so.

7. Do we today discriminate against people because of their sex, race or religion? Give examples.

GLOSSARY

Allahabad. City in North India in the south-east of Uttar Pradesh province where the Ganges and Jumna Rivers meet. Jawaharlal Nehru was born there.

American Civil War. The war fought from 1861 to 1865 betwen the northern and southern states of America.

Bhoonjal. A dry curry mix.

Bigan. A vegetable also known as aubergine or egg plant.

Bill. A rough outline of a law before it becomes an Act of Parliament.

Black-eyed peas. A bean grown in the tropics which has black markings on its skin.

Boston Tea Party. A raid in 1773 by citizens of Boston (disguised as Native Americans) who boarded three British ships in the harbour as a protest against taxes on tea and the exclusive control given to the East India Company to sell tea. The contents of several hundred chests of tea were dumped into the harbour.

Cassava. A root vegetable. It is an important food in the tropics. Tapioca is made from the starch-like quality in cassava.

Cast-nets. A net used for catching fish.

Caste. Any group of people sharing similar ways of living and working and whose whole way of life is shaped by the work the group does or by its wealth. In India there are four main castes, the Brahmin, Kshatriya, Vaisya and Sudra, into which Hindu people are divided.

Communist. A person who supports communism which is a system which wants to do away with companies, farms and other industries being owned by only a few people and let everybody own these things.

Constitution. The basic laws and rules by which a state is governed.

Dhal. Lentils or dried beans and peas which are eaten daily in almost every Indian home and which are often the only type of protein which poor people can afford to buy.

Demerara. A river in Guyana which rises in the central forest area and flows north to the Atlantic at Georgetown.

East Indian. An immigrant to the West Indies who is of Indian origin.

Emergency Regulations. Laws passed for a period of time to overcome a period of crisis. Normal rights of speech, to come and go as we like are suspended.

Essequibo. A river in Guyana which rises near the Brazilian border and flows north to the Atlantic. This river drains over half of Guyana.

Fascism. A belief or movement which does not believe in people voting for the government they want to govern them.

Gandhi, Mohadas Karamchand. Known as Mahatma (1869-1948). Indian political leader.

He played a very important part in India's struggle for independence from Britain and was often imprisoned by the British because of this.

Hindi.	The language spoken in the central part of North India.
Hindu.	A person who believes in Hinduism which is the main religion of India.
Jim Crow Laws.	The method by which black and white people were kept apart in the United States.
Koh-i-nor.	A very large Indian diamond which has been part of the British crown jewels since 1849.
Manatee.	An animal which lives in the coastal waters of the West Indies, America and Africa. It looks like a whale and has a broad flat tail.
Nehru, Jawaharlal (1889-1964).	Indian statesman and leader. He was imprisoned several times by the British for the part he played in India's struggle for independence. He became the first prime

minister of the republic of India (1947-1964).

Okra. A green pod with white seeds which is eaten as a vegetable often in soups and stews.

Padi. Sometimes spelt paddy. Grains of rice with outer husks or coats.

Plantain. A tropical fruit which is like a large banana. It can be green or yellow. It is a basic or daily food in many tropical countries.

Proportional representation. A system by which at a general election, the whole country is one constituency and seats are won as a result of the total number of votes cast. In the 'first past the post' system, the country is divided into a number of constituencies and seats are won depending on the majority of votes cast in a particular constituency.

Sari. The traditional dress of the women of India. It is made of a very long narrow piece of cloth which is roped and tied around the body.

Social Sciences. The study of society and of the way in which each member of society is connected to other members.

Suffrage. The right to vote.

TB (tuberculosis). A disease which often affects the lungs.

Wattle. A way of building walls using twigs which are plastered with a mixture of clay, lime and water. Sometimes dung and chopped straw are also used.

OTHER BOOKS IN THE SERIES:

Marcus Garvey - A Biography ISBN 0 90452 119 1
Celebrates the life of Jamaica's National Hero and was first published to commemorate the centenary of his birth in 1985.
Marcus Garvey has left his influence on every aspect of life impacting on African people everywhere.

Two Lives - Mary Seacole and Florence Nightingale ISBN 0 904 521191 5
Two lives contrasts the lives of two Victorian heroines and shows how they overcame restrictions placed on them because of their sex, race and class. One white, the other black, both were equally dedicated in their desire to be of service to mankind and to be free.
This title was one of the first choices on the runners-up list in the Primary Age Group for the coveted Times Educational Book Award in 1993.
The Biographical Series was welcomed by Mark Williamson in his review in the TES Book Awards, where he noted that '...individual lives were an important part of the tapestry that we call history...'

The Series is assessed as suitable for the Upper Primary and Lower secondary age groups. Teachers will find the glossary and questions invaluable teaching aids.